Skyscrapers
Record Breakers

Carmel Reilly

Skyscrapers: Record Breakers

Text: Carmel Reilly
Publishers: Tania Mazzeo and Eliza Webb
Series consultant: Amanda Sutera
  Hands on Heads Consulting
Editor: Laken Ballinger
Project editor: Annabel Smith
Designer: Leigh Ashforth
Project designer: Danielle Maccarone
Permissions researcher: Catherine Kerstjens
Production controller: Renee Tome

Acknowledgements
We would like to thank the following for permission to reproduce
copyright material:

Front cover: iStock.com/Nikada; pp. 1, 9 (inset): Alamy Stock Photo/Dennis
Hallinan; pp. 3, 14: Shutterstock.com/FiledIMAGE; p. 4: Shutterstock.
com/Scalia Media; p. 5: Martin Sanders © Cengage Learning Australia; p. 6
(top): Alamy Stock Photo/FAY 2018, (bottom): Photo by Jack E Boucher
from Prints and Photographs Division, Library of Congress (HABS NY,31-
NEYO,71--13); p. 7 (main): Shutterstock.com/Mulevich, (inset): Alamy Stock
Photo/Radharc Images; pp. 8, 24: Shutterstock.com/Felix Lipov; p. 9
(main): Shutterstock.com/Paper Cat; p. 10: Shutterstock.com/Rudy
Balasko; p. 11 (main): Alamy Stock Photo/Raymond Deleon, (inset): Getty
Images/Loop Images; p. 12: iStock.com/zorazhuang; p. 13 (main): iStock.
com/tampatra, (inset): iStock.com/tang90246; p. 15 (main): Shutterstock.
com/jax10289, (inset): Fairfax Syndication/Sebastian Costanzo; p. 16:
Shutterstock.com/Steven Bostock; p. 17 (main): Shutterstock.com/RAW-
films, (inset): Shutterstock.com/VladyslaV Travel photo; p. 18, back cover:
iStock.com/Dylan Rogers; p. 19: Shutterstock.com/Rasto SK; p. 20 (main):
iStock.com/f9photos, (inset): iStock.com/LanaStock; p. 21 (top): iStock.
com/MesquitaFMS, (middle): iStock.com/CHUNYIP WONG, (bottom):
iStock.com/Edwin Tan; p. 22 (top): iStock.com/pixelheadphoto, (second
from top): Getty Images/Donald Iain Smith, (third from top): iStock.
com/LanaStock, (bottom): Shutterstock.com/Cristian Zamfir.

Every effort has been made to trace and acknowledge copyright.
However, if any infringement has occurred, the publishers tender their
apologies and invite the copyright holders to contact them.

NovaStar

Text © 2024 Cengage Learning Australia Pty Limited

ISBN 978 0 17 033417 4

Cengage Learning Australia
Level 5, 80 Dorcas Street
Southbank VIC 3006 Australia
Phone: 1300 790 853
Email: aust.nelsonprimary@cengage.com

For learning solutions, visit **cengage.com.au**

Printed in China by 1010 Printing International Ltd
1 2 3 4 5 6 7 28 27 26 25 24

*Nelson acknowledges the Traditional Owners and Custodians
of the lands of all First Nations Peoples. We pay respect
to Elders past and present, and extend that respect to
all First Nations Peoples today.*

Contents

Skyscrapers

Skyscrapers are very tall buildings that are at least 150 metres high and have 40 floors or more. The first skyscrapers were built in the late 1800s in the USA. They were created to make extra space in crowded cities. Since then, thousands of skyscrapers have been **constructed** all over the world.

One hundred years ago, the tallest skyscraper was around 240 metres high. This is about the same height as 40 two-storey houses stacked on top of each other. Today, the tallest skyscraper is more than three times that height!

Busy cities like New York City, USA, have lots of skyscrapers to make room for all the people who live there.

But skyscrapers are more than just the tallest buildings in the world. They are also places where people live, work and visit.

Tall, Supertall and Megatall

There are three types of skyscrapers. "Tall" skyscrapers are more than 150 metres high. "Supertall" skyscrapers are more than 300 metres high, and "megatall" skyscrapers are more than 600 metres high! Today, there are thousands of tall and supertall skyscrapers in the world. However, there are only four megatall skyscrapers in the world.

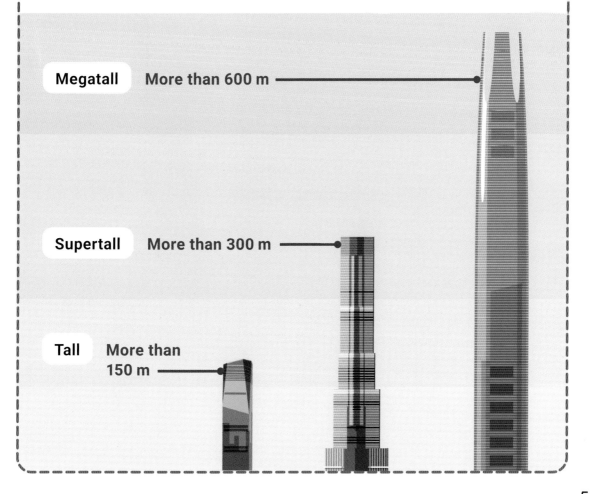

Megatall   **More than 600 m**

Supertall   **More than 300 m**

Tall   **More than 150 m**

The Singer Building

Location » New York City, USA

Building time » 2 years

Year of opening » 1908

Height » 184 metres

Floors » 47

Lifts » 16

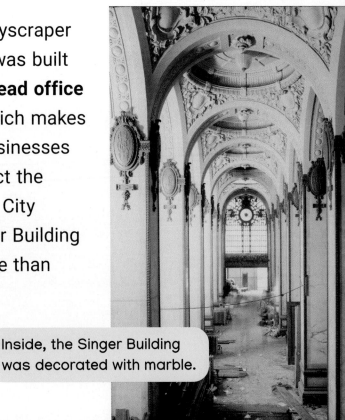

The Singer Building had a wider base and a tall tower at the top.

The world's first modern skyscraper was the Singer Building. It was built from 1906 to 1908 as the **head office** for the Singer Company, which makes sewing machines. Many businesses were competing to construct the tallest building in New York City around this time. The Singer Building was the first one to be more than 150 metres high, but it was only the tallest building in the city for one year!

Inside, the Singer Building was decorated with marble.

Tall Shadows

The **architect** who **designed** the Singer Building, Ernest Flagg, thought that tall buildings blocked sunlight and made city streets dark and cold. He tried to avoid this when he planned the Singer Building. He made the building's tower quite narrow and set it back from the street so that it would not **overshadow** its neighbours.

Tall buildings can create shadows on city streets.

The Singer Building was **demolished** in 1968 to make way for a much bigger skyscraper. At the time, it was the tallest building to ever be pulled down.

A new skyscraper, called One Liberty Plaza, was built in the place where the Singer Building used to be.

The Empire State Building

Location » New York City, USA

Building time » 14 months

Year of opening » 1931

Height » 443 metres (including radio **antenna**)

Floors » 102

Lifts » 73

The Empire State Building is a symbol of New York City.

The Empire State Building is famous for its beautiful **design** and its tall **spire**. It was the world's tallest building for 40 years, from 1931 to 1971.

The Empire State Building was the first skyscraper to have more than 100 floors. It also has enough office space for more than 10 000 people. The building is so large that it even has its own **zip code**!

The top of the Empire State Building gives visitors a bird's-eye view of New York City.

Large numbers of people visit the building's **observation decks** on the 86th and 102nd floors. About 4 million tourists come to see the view of New York City from the top every year.

Lightning!

The radio antenna on the very top of the Empire State Building's spire is hit by lightning around 25 times a year.

The Willis Tower

Location » Chicago, USA

Building time » 3 years

Year of opening » 1973

Height » 442 metres

Floors » 110

Lifts » 103

The Willis Tower is unusual compared to other skyscrapers because it is black.

The Willis Tower is an office building, and it was the world's tallest skyscraper for almost 25 years, from 1973 to 1996. It is still the tallest building in Chicago.

The Willis Tower is covered in black metal and 16 000 dark-coloured glass windows. It has two 85-metre-tall antennas on its roof. More than 50 local TV and radio stations use these antennas to **broadcast** different programs.

The Willis Tower observation deck has a glass floor.

Inside, the Willis Tower has over 400 000 square metres of floor space. That is about the size of 56 soccer fields! The observation deck, which is on the 103rd floor, is the highest in the USA.

Cleaning Windows

The windows on the Willis Tower are cleaned eight times a year by special **robotic** window cleaning machines that can be rolled down from the roof.

robotic window cleaners

The Petronas Twin Towers

Location » Kuala Lumpur, Malaysia

Building time » 7 years

Year of opening » 1999

Height » 452 metres

Floors » 88

Lifts » 39 in each tower

The Petronas Twin Towers were built as office space for the Petronas oil company. "Twin towers" are two buildings that have the same design and are built side by side. The twin towers in Malaysia are the tallest in the world. It takes two months to clean all the windows in both towers!

The Petronas Twin Towers were built to look exactly the same.

Traditional Shapes

The design of the Petronas Twin Towers is based on shapes often found in Malaysian art, such as stars.

a bird's-eye view of the Petronas Twin Towers

Although the Petronas Twin Towers are separate buildings, a skybridge connects them between the 41st and 42nd floors. This skybridge is two storeys tall and is 170 metres above the ground. It was built so that people could easily move from one tower to another. It also helps to keep the towers from shaking too much in strong winds.

The skybridge is the highest two-storey bridge in the world.

The Eureka Tower

Location » Melbourne, Australia

Building time » 4 years

Year of opening » 2006

Height » 297 metres

Floors » 92

Lifts » 13

One of Australia's well-known skyscrapers is the Eureka Tower, which is an apartment building in Melbourne. It was the tallest building in Australia for 14 years, from 2006 until 2020. It was also the world's tallest apartment building from 2006 to 2010.

At the very top of the Eureka Tower are some gold windows. These were put there to remind people of the gold that was found in Australia in the 1800s.

The Eureka Tower is beside the Yarra River, which runs through Melbourne.

Visitors can see the highest view of Melbourne from the Eureka Tower observation deck.

The Eureka Tower has an observation deck on its 88th floor. This deck has a special cube made entirely of glass, which can slide in and out from the side of the building. When the cube slides out, people standing on the glass floor can see straight through it to the ground, almost 300 metres below!

Race to the Top

A stair-climbing race called the Eureka Climb is held at the tower every year. Racers run from the ground floor all the way to the 88th floor. The fastest time recorded is 7 minutes and 34 seconds!

The Burj Khalifa

Location » Dubai, United Arab Emirates

Building time » 6 years

Year of opening » 2010

Height » 828 metres

Floors » 163

Lifts » 57

The Burj Khalifa looks as if it is made from several towers put together.

The Burj Khalifa (say: *burge kah-lee-fah*) is a megatall skyscraper. When the outside of the tower was finished in 2009, the Burj Khalifa became the tallest megatall skyscraper and the tallest building in the world by more than 300 metres!

The Burj Khalifa holds a number of world records for skyscrapers. As of 2023, it has:

→ the most floors of any building

→ the world's highest outdoor observation deck

→ the world's longest distance lift ride.

The observation deck on the Burj Khalifa is on the 124th floor.

Every day, almost one million litres of water are pumped into the Burj Khalifa for use in its kitchens, bathrooms and **air-conditioning system**. That is about half the amount of water in an Olympic-size swimming pool. The building's **solar panels** make electricity to heat all of this water.

What a Trip!

It only takes one minute for a lift in the Burj Khalifa to travel 500 metres up, the distance between the ground floor and the 124th floor. People may feel their ears pop when they ride the lift!

The Shard

Location » London, UK

Building time » 4 years

Year of opening » 2012

Height » 310 metres

Floors » 95

Lifts » 44

The Shard is shaped differently from other buildings and looks like a giant shard, or piece, of glass.

The Shard is the tallest building in the UK and the seventh tallest in Europe.

The Shard's design is quite different from other skyscrapers. It looks like a tall pyramid with an uneven spiky top. The outside is covered in 11 000 **panes** of glass, which **reflect** the colour of the sky at different times of the day.

The Shard includes offices, a hotel, apartments and a **TV studio**. It has the UK's highest observation deck, which is on the 72nd floor. Around one million people visit the deck every year.

Amazing Skyscrapers

Skyscrapers are built to create new spaces for people to live and work. They often have unusual designs, and many of them have broken records for how high a building can be constructed.

Skyscrapers truly are amazing buildings that create more space in crowded cities!

Skyscrapers:

Do We Really Need More of Them in Our City?

> As we know, a lot of cities have skyscrapers. But is it a good idea to keep building them here in our city? Carlos and Clarissa, what do you two think?

Reporter

Cities around the world build skyscrapers as places for people to live, work and play.

I think that skyscrapers are a great idea in crowded cities. They give us extra space for living and working. Many of them are also incredible to look at. Some people say that skyscrapers are not good for the environment, but lots of them are now built with solar panels and water recycling systems. Building more skyscraper apartment buildings here will provide more homes for people. I think that is a good thing.

Skyscrapers can have solar panels on their roofs to make electricity for the building.

Skyscrapers provide homes to lots of people.

Clarissa

It can be hard to get fresh air or enjoy the outdoors when living in a skyscraper.

66 We don't need more skyscrapers. Because of their size, they often block sunlight, and their shadows make the city cold and dark. Some skyscrapers look great, but most are just huge metal towers that use too much electricity. Lots of skyscrapers don't even have balconies, gardens or windows that open. Many people don't like working or living high off the ground. Let's just have smaller buildings. 99

Reporter

Skyscrapers should be good for both a city's environment and its people.

66 Thank you, Carlos and Clarissa. Perhaps we don't really need more skyscrapers. But if we do build them, they should be environmentally friendly. Otherwise, having a range of different kinds of buildings in the city is the best idea. 99

Glossary

air–conditioning system (*noun*)
a machine that cools the air inside a building

antenna (*noun*)
a wire made out of metal that can send and receive signals from a radio or TV

architect (*noun*)
someone who plans how a building will look

broadcast (*verb*)
to send out a signal on radio or TV

constructed (*verb*)
built or made

demolished (*verb*)
knocked down (a building)

design (*noun*)
the shape of a building and how it looks

designed (*verb*)
planned how something should look

head office (*noun*)
the main place where people in a company work together

observation decks (*noun*)
floors in buildings that are used to look out at a view

overshadow (*verb*)
to cause a shadow to fall over something

panes (*noun*)
sheets of glass that are used for windows

reflect (*verb*)
to bounce back light or pictures from a mirror or window

solar panels (*noun*)
devices that use heat and light from the Sun to make electricity

spire (*noun*)
a tall structure on the top of a building

TV studio (*noun*)
a place where TV shows are made

zip code (*noun*)
a number that is used as part of an address in the USA, like a post code

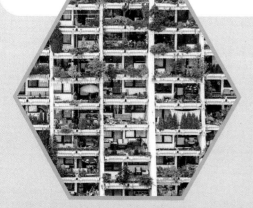

Index